# THE
# ROYAL
# PARCHMENT
# SCROLL
# OF
# BLACK
# SUPREMACY

by
Rev. Fitz Balintine Pettersburgh
with Prologue by
Ras Miguel Lorne.

The **Queen of Queens** of Ethiopia,
**Empress Menen** with two of the
pupils at the Girls High School
that she founded.

Printed in the USA

ISBN 0-94839-076-X

Distributed by:
Frontline Books
751 East 75th Street
Chicago, IL 60619
USA
Tel: (773) 651-9888
Fax: (773) 651-9850
Email: frontlinebooks@hotmail.com

Distributed in the Eastern Caribbean by:
Frontline Books
PO Box 956 E
Eagle Hall
St. Michael, Barbados
Tel: (246) 228-1770

Co-Published in Jamaica
Miguel Lorne Publishers
PO Box 2967
Kingston, Jamaica
Tel: (876) 922-3915

II

# CONTENTS

# ISES FOR THE VICTORY

*Natural in Thy glory*
*Oh **JAH RASTAFARI***
*I-N-I will For Iver Praise Thee,*
*for there is none*
*neither under the earth,*
*or over the earth,*
*nor within the earth*
*more worthy of Praises*
*than the AMLIGHTY I- **JAH***
***RASTAFARI.***

*For I-N-I have seen your*
*dungeons,*
*we have seen your*
*prisons,*
*we have suffered for the cause*
*and have survived*
*all your tribulations*
*But in the Igesty of His Majesty*
*I-N-I must stand*
*to Praise the Living I Am,*
*So trod on my people*
*trod on,*
*fight on my people*
*fight on,*
*Move up my people*
*move up,*
*for together we are strong*

*IV*

*And our JAH,*
*The BLACK JAH of all Creation*
*will vanquish the wicked and Itect (protect)*
*the Righteous,*
*Now and For Iver more*
*Dreadlocks*
***JAH RASTAFARI***
***JAH RASTAFARI***
***JAH RASTAFARI....***

# WORDS OF THE I MAJESTY

Education develops the intellect; and the intellect distinguishes man from other creatures. It is Education that enables man to harness nature and utilise her resources for the well-being and improvement of his life. The key for the betterment and completeness of modern living is education.

But, *"Man cannot live by bread alone"*. Man after all, is also composed of intellect and soul. Therefore, education in general and higher education in particular, must aim to provide, beyond the physical food for intellect and soul. That education which ignores man's intrinsic nature and neglects his intellect and reasoning power cannot be considered true education.

A well organised education should not be one which prepares students for a food remuneration alone. It should be one that can help and guide them towards acquiring clear thinking, a fruitful mind and an elevated spirit.

The educated person that Ethiopia and countries of her level need is not one who has stuffed bits of knowledge into his mind. The needed educated individual is one who uses the ideas he obtained from his lectures, books, and discussions to the best advantage of his own country and his own people. It is he who disseminates new ideas in harmony with economic and social aspects of his own community so that fruitful results will be realised. This is the person who can show segments of knowledge he accumulated in his own learning, inventiveness in a new situation.

Ethiopia is a country with her own culture and mores. These, our cultures and customs, more than being the legacy of our historical past, are characteristic of our Ethiopianness.

*We do not want our legacies and traditions to be lost. Our wish and desire is that education develops, enrich, and modify them.*

*You all know the continuous effort that Ethiopia is exerting for the development of profound and high persons for research, or the study and development of our country's resources, for technology, for medicine, for law, and the administration of our people according to their customs. These are the needs that constrain us to provide, at all levels, education free of charge. And students, ever mindful of this privilege, should endeavour to recompense their country and nation.*

*The opportunity for education, afforded to the few in our country, is not given to them for a fashion or a mode. It is given for a purpose, for a task, for a high responsibility, for full and exhaustive use, for the benefit of our country, and the coming generation.*

*We have just explained to you the type of result and responsibility that we expect from you students. It is on you, the members of the Faculty that we must rely for this result. We realise the heavy responsibility we have entrusted to you. We hope that you too while believing and accepting your responsibilities as your sacred duties, will produce for Ethiopia, persons who take pride in you and their education and are ready for the call of service.*

*It is you who must mould the minds of your students - that they may be wise, farsighted, intelligent, profound in their thinking, devoted to their country and government and fruitful in their work.*

*It is you who must serve as the example. On their part also, they will have to learn not only formal education but also self-discipline that should be worthy to be inherited. May the Almighty God be with you in the fulfillment of your duties.*

# Front cover Itrate (Picture)

This is a reprint of a front cover, printed in Rastafari Speaks 1st reissue 2002, showing the pope prostrating to the I Majesty- Emperor Haile Sellassie I, the earth's Rightful ruler.

To most Rastafarians, this Ipicts (depicts) the Pope bowing to the Almighty I AM- Haile I as King and God.

When the Pope bows to the I Majesty, it demonstrates the power of good over evil, right over wrong, the victory of the down-pressed over the down-pressor.

InI think that this cover is relevant and most appropriate for this time, when the Hola Order of the Nyabinghi stands Predominate in Babylon; whilst Rome and all who worships her must bow before the Black Gods and Goddesses, the sons and daughters of the Most High and noble one. Emperor Haile Sellassie and Empress Menen. JAH RASTAFARI! King Rastafari liveth for Iver. African liberation is soon approaching it's final frontier. Hence, InI, i.e. all African man and woman must strive to become each other's keeper, both at home and abroad.

African people, stop serving and worshiping strange and false gods, and start worshiping in our own image and likeness- Our Black God and King- The I Majesty Emperor Haile Sellassie I as King of Kings and Lord of Lords.

Feb' 03 Ras Sekou T.

# *Prologue*

This ancient teachings of The ALMIGHTY is written upon the Heart and through the Natural Doctrine of Faith, Man has transcended to the Celestial Realms within His Majesty's inner sanctuary, there to be blessed and receive Itinual Honour.

The Almighty is so great, that He does not expect I-N-I to be HIM. All He asks is that we pursue perfection and righteousness and all things shall be added unto I-N-I. The pursuit of it, is satisfactory to Him, much more the attainments.

Natural in thy Glory, Oh **JAH RASTAFARI.**

In the 1490's the carrying of black people from Africa to the Western Hemisphere began. What turned out to be a brutal and prolonged enslavement was on its way. The aim was to separate the greatest minds from the greatest land. That perpetual divide, has haunted us, even unto this day. Over here in the West we have the Creative abilities and the genius minds, but no collateral to back it up, and so many of our people must devote their brilliant minds to those who have collateral - the slave masters.
In Africa all the resources are there, but many people are physically in Africa, whilst their minds are in Mecca, Russia, Europe or America.

It has been a cycle of endless toil in the West with only the crumbs from the exploiters table being deliberately dropped for the comedians, the lackeys, the sportsmen, the traitors and those who have bowed to them. The Rebels, the Resisters, and the Unrepentant face perpetual hardships and persecutions.

The black Revolts, Rebellions, Uprisings and **Wars,**
dented the pride of the downpressors. But they lacked
cohesion and the back-a-tive of a strong Fatherland.

The tactics have changed; the chains have been
removed from the feet and placed on the brains. So the
enslavement now is easier and offer less responsibilities
for the Owners.

In 1884 the White world gathered at the Berlin
Conference and planned how they would over-power
and share up Africa without offending each other.
Part of the plan was the capture of Ethiopia. They knew
that Ethiopia was the Black man's pride, The
Blackmans crowning glory and the seat of Zion. They
desperately wanted the Ark-of-the-Covenant, the Throne
House of the ALMIGHTY.

IN 1889 Emperor Yohannes died in battle at Metemma
whilst defending Ethiopia from the Muslim Invaders.
Despite the loss of their Emperor, the Ethiopians
succeeded in maintaining their Independence and won a
resounding Victory over the Muslims.

The Muslims did not cease trying, and with the Italians
on the other hand pursuing their own goals of capture,
the Ethiopians had their hands full in regular and
continuos battles.

With the birth of our Lord and Saviour JAH RASTAFARI
in July 1892, the enemies decided that they would
implement all-out attacks in an effort to destroy the
Christ - child whilst He was still a baby.
Thus in 1894 the Muslims came and again was soundly
defeated. But the greatest victory came at the Battle of
Adowa on the 1st of March 1896, when the Romans
were convincingly destroyed.

*XII*

This Ethiopian Victory was more than a Military success It was the victory of the Red, Gold and Green over the red, white and blue. A victory of JAH RASTAFARI over the Pope and Vatican. Victory of Good over evil. Victory of the Lamb over the beast. Endless praises to the Almighty I- *JAH RASTAFARI*.

The Victory of the Ethiopians was a source for Black Pride in the World, and at the turn of the Century there was a strong and powerful surge for Black Dignity, Self-assertion and Independence.

In territories such as Jamaica, Haiti, Cuba, Brazil and parts of the Americas, our brothers and sisters took to the hills, so as to withdraw their labour. This hurt the downpressors to the core as it meant a serious dwindling of profits and which led to the economic collapse of the Western Economies in the 1930's.

Whereas the white-man was a Trespasser in Africa, the feeling was different over here. He felt that this was his domain and seeing that we were separated from our roots and the numerous atrocities we had gone through, that we should be sub-servient. After all, they had taken away our name, our religion, our culture, our women, and murdered many of the Rebels Therefore any talk like "skin for skin" "colour for colour", "death to white and black downpressors" was seen as Sedition and Treason and brothers and sisters were harshly punished. In this, the colonial rulers were proudly assisted by those "well learned" gentle men, most of whom were Traitors. Despite the overbearing persecutions and torments here in Jamaica there were some strong Black Leaders who preached and wrote BLACK SUPREMACY in all its Majestical Glory.

Brothers such as MARCUS GARVEY, LEONARD HOWELL, ALEXANDER BEDWARD, J.A. ROGERS, MANTLE,COOMBS, ROBERT RUMBLE, BUCHANNAN and many others.

They were not trained at the babylon Colleges and Universities but graduated from Universities of the Streets - the peoples University.
They haunted the citadel of evil - the heart of the City Kingston at places such as, out-side Ward Theatre, Coke Church steps, at the Chigger-Foot Market, at Redemption Ground, Oxford Street, Darling Street, Coronation Markets etc. with their dazzling Sunday evening meetings. The crowds were large and the oratory was brilliant. Because they were often facing persecutions, they used the Court House to declare their principles and made scathing attacks upon the whiteman, knowing that the guilty verdict already put down.
Apart from the Government and police, there was another vicious enemy of the people - the Gleaner Newspaper.

It is out of these struggles that the Rastafari Movement re-incarnated in Jamaica. Many of the early Rastafarians, out of fear, did not dreadlocks and were very apprehensive to keep a little beard.
A passage from the Gleaner sums up the Colonial attitude.

*"They refrained from shaving; their chins became bearded, so much so that a few person of higher intelligence incurred the risk of prosecution for assault, when they held some of these deluded creatures and scraped the hair from their faces."*

This passage was taken from the Gleaner of the 6th August 1934. Persons who openly broke the law and violated the human rights of others were seen as of "higher intelligence" and those who were fulfilling the principles of their faith were called "deluded creatures" How much more disrespectful could Gleaner get.

The unwritten Law of Jamaica in the 1920s, thirties & forties became the written Law of Dominica in the 1970s when the Dread Act gave police and citizens the right to shoot a Rastafarian on sight. Dominicas honour will be forever scarred by this most droconian piece of legislation, certainly one of the worst in this century in the Western Hemisphere.

Locks and beards were seen as an affront and open violation to the system. So you can imagine how they felt when the brothers were preaching the "Black God" concept.

In fact the system was doing everything to wipe out this philosophy and its adherents. Another passage from the Gleaner will explain it better than I can.

**"It is learnt that due to the activity of the St. Thomas police, Ras-Tafarians have been brought to a stand-still in that parish. They are not permitted to hold meetings and speak in support of the doctrine they expouse. For the present the movement which was started in St. Thomas a couple of years ago has ceased to exist."**

You can imagine how much internal hatred is being fostered each time they see I-N-I. As far as they are concerned, we 'ceased to exist'.

The laws of the country supported those "persons of higher intelligence".

Prior to the 20th Century there was a law in Jamaica which provided exclusive privileges to the Chinese, Syrians, Jews, Whites etc. to control and monopolize the wholesale and Retail Trade. This law made it clear that Black People could not "Re-vend" and therefore we could only sell what we produce that is fowls, provisions, fish and milk. The result of this law is visible today, in that if you go to the Coronation Market, it is black people that is seen selling ground provisions, fish, fowls, etc. Whilst the Chinese, Syrians, Jews, and Whites control the wholesale and Retail trades with their stores, supermarkets, etc.

Most of us grow up in areas where the 'Chinese' shops were very successful whilst the 'Black Shops' struggled Consequently a feeling developed that 'Black man can't keep shop'. This myth came about because of the laws that existed for the protection of the Chinese and White shops and the credit monopoly they enjoyed. Therefore it was not enough to simply abolish these laws, because their fruits exist today. What must be done is that the same way the Chinese, Syrians, Whites and Jews etc. were given special privileges, it is only fair that Black People be given special treatment for a period of time.
It is against these type of laws and their perpetrators that the advocates of Black Supremacy had to struggle to attain and assert BLACKNESS.

It is out of this climate that the Royal Parchment Scroll of ⁿlack Supremacy emerged.

It pointed to the Blackness of God. It asserted our homeland Ethiopia and it challenged the western Christian Status quo of the Adam - Abraham - Anglo - Saxon ring. Once again the Gleaner is most apt in showing the "masters" contempt for a book that proudly asserts blackness. An article on the 6th of June 1927 states in regard to **The Royal Parchment Scroll of Black Supremacy:-**

> *'The grammar is like the sense,*
> *which seems to us to be indistinguishable from*
> *nonsense, and the whole concoction is so putrid*
> *that we wonder what class of people could ever*
> *take such rubbish seriously'.*

Despite this, there were a very large 'class of people' that took it ously.
Even unto s day there are many who thirst for the book. One of the factors that prompted I to reprint and publish this book was the large amount of people on a regular basis that keep coming to **Headstart Book Shop** asking for this book. So much so, that when it became apparent that the book would soon be available we had orders in excess of a thousand copies. So there seem. be a very large "class of people" that do take this "rubbish" seriously.

Many of the elders I spoke to keep referring to Balintine as valentine, and they make reference to several meetings between himself and Leonard Howell, one of the first exponent of Rastafari. Especially a meeting in October 1933 whereby they attacked "Ministers of the Gospel, also churches and white men".
In September of 1924 Rev. Fitz Balintine Pettersburgh arrived in Jamaica from the United States.

The Royal Parchment Scroll of Black Supremacy was published about June of 1926. It was part of an "encyclopedia" which was prepared for publication from as early as July of 1925.

**The Royal Parchment Scroll of Black Supremacy** in its early form was set out like a bible with Chapters and Verses etc.

This is a reflection of the thinking of the time, as it was known that many people only accept the "gospel" if it is presented in a biblical manner.

The contents of the "Scroll" are strong and penetrating.
**Black Supremacy is-**
**"the queen of Ethiopia's Triumphant Resurrection Africa's desire is to rebuild Solomon's temple, but Solomon is not big enough, Nor his father David to dictate to the Monarch of DREAD CREATION",**
I-N-I the Rastafarian interpret the 'Monarch of Dread Creation' to mean His Imperial Majesty - **JAH RASTAFARI.**
Rev. Balintine entreated the people:
**'do not follow Court House and Doctors they will fake you to death.'**
His love and admiration for his wife is to be emulated by all Africans. With respect to her he said:-
**'Lady Pettersburgh the perfect Mrs. of Black Supremacy is my wife, your mother is a perfect lady.'**

It would appear that it was a problem then as it is now with his admonishing of certain men not to:-

> *'breed up the young girls, and treat them like dogs. Every good looking man's wife you see, you want to cohabit with her, you rotten gut snake.'*

Rev. Balintines loyalty to the King of Kings was overwhelming and he closes with the words-

> *"And take off the Black Man from off the Anglo-Saxon Slave Train that hour. Christianity and Civilisation is now Black Supremacy".*

The important factor about **The Royal Parchment Scroll of Black Supremacy** is not whether readers accept all that he has stated but that he was bold enough to put them forward and challenge the Colonial rulers at their religious sources.

Religion is the tool used for Centuries by the white man to brainwash and trick I-N-I.

**The Royal Parchment Scroll** will help to burst the bubble and assist in Liberating our minds.

*JAH LOVE*

*Ras Miguel Lorne*

# The Royal Parchment Scroll

# of  Black  Supremacy

---

## Author:  Rev. Fitz Balintine Pettersburgh

## Date: ca. June 1926

# Place: Kingston, Jamaica

---

**The Royal Parchment  Scroll of Black
Supremacy**

*Our eternal Life Creator The Owner of
Life, The Eternal Register Office
K.A.Q.O., The Crown
Register General Office Black Supremacy
The Church Triumphant, The Crown Law of
Education & Sacred Theocracy
K.A.Q.O.S.W.J.W., The Monarch Documents*

*(Protect all), Human Descriptions
K.O.K.... The Black man is The Master of
this World, Theocracy, The Dictionary,
Law Courts & Money Mints & Governments*

3

*K.A.Q.O....* The *world's* *first* *Triumphant* *Capital, The Isle of Spring, The*

*Triumphant Bible Land, King*

*Alpha and Queen Omega Black Folks......*

*His & Her Copyright of Creation,*

One of the portable gallows carried round to the villages to liquidate the Elders: another photograph taken by the Italians of their own crimes in Ethiopia

4

*The Lion & His Lioness & Baby, His & Her*

*Arch Dynasty of Holy Time, His Tri-*

*Divinity & Her Tri-Virginity, His & Her*

*Arch Monarchy, His & Her Majesty Queen*

*Lula May Fitz Balintine Petersburgh*

*K.O.K., A.D. 1926, Mt.*

*Africa,     The     Throne,     Ethiopian     Bible
Owner*

*A.B.C.(1)*

---

(1) The opening text in italics indicate the material that was written in a careful scroll surrounding the outside of the book cover.

# *INTRODUCTION*

My dear inhabitants of this world, we are the foundation stones of the resurrection of the Kingdom of Ethiopia.

Our prayers and labour for your resurrection is past finding out. No Library in this world is able to contain the work of our hands for you.

For we work day and night for your Deliverance.

As for this generation of the 20th Century, you have no knowledge how worlds are built.

And upon what trigger Kingdoms are set.

In my Encyclopedia I will explain to you all, how worlds are being built and what triggers Kingdoms are set on.

I will also explain to you, the Capacities of generations.

Speaking for the Universe, and the Womanhood of Man, I the Ethiopian woman, is the Crown woman of the world.

Without any apology, to any mortal that was ever created by King Alpha and Omega.

I hand you my Rule Book from the poles of Supreme Authority.

**I AM** THE CANON MISTRESS OF CREATION.

Kingston, Jamaica

B.W.I. Tropic of Cancer

July 15th 1925, A.D.

Rev Fitz Balintine Pettersburgh, King of Kings, Creator of Theocracy, and Biblical Sovreign. The Crown Head of Holy Time, A.B.C.-S.J.W.

# ETHIOPIA'S PREFACE

The preface of this Rule Book, is the Finger Post, into the Kingdom of Ethiopia.
Ethiopia is the Succeeding Kingdom of the Angle Saxon kingdom.
Our philosopher is the Angle Saxon Philosopher's (Successor), a wide awake Universal Master Mind.

A man of greater learning is not found on the face of the Globe. A swifter thinker is God Almighty A better Christian Soul and King Alpha and Omega. Women must be proud of good men, when they are right on the job.
Men must be proud of us Women when we can deliver able Sons and Daughters to the Four Poles of the Globe.

And make the Nations Hearts rejoice with raging joy. We give God the Glory.

THE CROWN MISTRESS THE THRONE LAW-GIVER.
His & Her Majesty King Alpha and Queen Omega, COPYRIGHT.
His & Her Dynasty Queen Lula may Fitz Balintine Pettersburgh, S.J.W.,A .B.C. Ph.D.,L.L.,K.O.K.

8

# ETHIOPIA'S FLY LEAF

ROYAL AIR MOUNT. I am going to teach the
Princess to fly around the poles.

PHILOSOPHERS.-- Brother Pettersburgh and
Sister Lula may Butler.

CLERGYMEN.-- Bible Owner, Lexium, and
Money Mint.
My Perfect Air Mount is Black Supremacy,
The Church Triumphant.
My Dynasty is the Triumphant Dynasty.

We are King Alpha and Queen Omega, THE
PAYMASTERS of the World.
Do not forget we are Black Supremacy.
A.B.C. Post Graduates
.J.W.K.A.Q.O.K.O.K.

Chapter 1

# THE ETHIOPIAN WESTERN REPOSITORY

Now, this is the morning of our resurrection therefore, we the Royal Tree, are very busy, cleaning up our Ancient and Modern Royal right away from Pole to Pole.
And the preparing of Guests for the Coronation.

THE CORONATION.-- The Coronation of Ethiopia's Postarities are as sure as the purity of pure gold.

THE CROWN MISTRESS .-- I Mrs. Indiana Coombs, being the Crown Mrs. of our Ethiopian Repository, for the Tropic of Cancer, I move the Crownship of the world right at this yard limit of time.
And present this generation of the 20th century my supreme Book of Royal Rules from the Ethiopian Western Repository.

## ILLUSTRATION

Owing to the Universal Rend of our Ancient and Modern Kingdoms, we are at this junction of our history scattered over the Globe into little Sectional groups commonly called Bands.

Ethiopian's Western Repository, is a strictly Christian Museum.

All our local bands throughout the globe, are bent towards this Royal Repository.

THE ROYAL AUTHORITY.-- This Official Bill of Royal Authority, is to admit all Bands, Missions, Camps, Denominations, into this Supreme Royal Repository.

THE BALMING MISTRESS.—
I being the Balming Mistress of many worlds I charge the Power-House right now.

## *THE RULE BOOK*

The Rule Book leads you into different department of the Kingdom.
The Records of the Kingdom are with us, unto this day.
The regulations, points you to the baseses of the Kingdom.

Chapter 2

## THE ROYAL MOVE

THE ROYAL MOVE

We move at the Signal of the Trumpet by Degrees call Bands.The Names of the Bands all over the Globe are too numerous to be named.

The Supreme Band, is Officially called the Royal Angel Band. The Royal Angel Band is the Crown Band of the world.

THE SEAL OF THE BAND.-- The seal of the Royal Angel Band, is the SAMARITAN Woman that needed the pity of Jesus (the well of Samaria)The Order and degree of this Fighting Line is after the Baptism of Jesus, into the Kingdom, by John the Baptist in the Royal River Jordan.

THE SUPREME SIGNAL.-- The Supreme Signal is the Official Signal of the (Holy Dove), as she moved from the Mercy Seat and Rested upon King Jesus Head at His Baptism in the Great River Jordan. see Matthew's 3:13.(2)

THE WELL OF SAMARIA.--the Woman at first refused to obey the request of Our Lord because she was spiritually blind.

---

(2)"Then cometh Jesus from Galilee to the Jordan unto John, to be baptized by him".

But when the Great physician opened up her eyes and HEALED her of her infirmities, concerning her many husbands in the City of Samaria, she found out that her five husbands were the five false teachers or denominations throughout the State or Country of Samaria.

Then she cried aloud unto the inhabitants of the city and said "Come see a man that told me all ever I did, and is not a Native of Samaria but an Hebrew, is not this man the very Christ"?

OUR CITIES OF TO-DAY.-- Our cities of to-day are inhabited with the self same qualities of people, as it was in the case of Jesus and the woman of Samaria.

Chapter 3

# THE HEALING PLOUGH OF CREATION

The healing plough of the Repository Transplanted and rebuild your very soul and body without fail.

THE MISERY OF THE LAND IS HEALED BY FASTING. We pick you up from out of the midst of the raging misery of the land and HIDE you from the raging Wolves of the land into our Balm Yard.

What is a Balm yard? A balm yard is a Holy place that is wholly consecrated to God Almighty for the cleansing and healing of the Nations. Where the Holy Spirit of God ALONE is ALLOWED to do the Royal Work of Healing.

(Ques.)   Who does the Balming work?
(Ans.) Consecrated men and women that the Holy Spirit moves, upon the Blazing Altar of their Souls, and endowed them with power that they command and handle the infirmities of the Nations.
(Ques) Have they any authority from God?
(Ans) Yes, we are vessels of the Divine Honour!

(Ques) Have you any authority from the World?
(Ans)    ASSUREDLY   YES   INDEED.   The Copyright of Theocracy signs for Our destiny   and   gave   us   His   supreme Affidavit for a Trillion centuries after the end of Eternal Life.

# ADMISSION TO THE BALM YARD

First and last every Soul for admission must believe in the power of the Living God.
Second an admission fee must be paid in advance, from one dollar up. According to the power and DURATION of the MISERABLE infirmities whereof one is afflicted.

SPECIAL NOTICE.
Sometimes I have to perform special medical attention.


THE REPOSITORY'S PROPER BODY.
According to the order of Melchisedec the Ethiopian Chief High Priest, we raise the Royal Banner on the top mass of the four poles of Creation, King Alpha and Queen Omega.

## Chapter 4

## *HER ROYAL BANQUET*

She brought me to her Banqueting House, and her Royal Banner over me, in her Royal Banquet Chamber is love.

THE WORKING OF THE BAND
The Band is a Royal encircling Band.
The Degree of this distinguished Band is a Royal Degree.
The (Encircling) "Staff Officers" are men and women of high spiritual ranks.

A Membership of six (Encircling), "Stax Officials" are sufficient for any one band of one hundred members.
Twenty-five members is one group.
That is one circle.
One circle, only needs one (Encircling) Staff Officer on the parade.

Along with the ORDAINED Circle Mother or Father by law, as many is are in the Banquet O.K.

## ROYAL NOTICE

Bands are not runned by Ministers. They are runned by the Priesthood, not after the Order of Aaron but strictly after the Royal Order of Melchisedec THE KING OF SALEM.

REVIVALISTS are not common people, if some individuals of the lower Order in the dung heap happen to get into the fold by mistake he or she will soon go out and hang him or herself.
The reason why, Revivalists World has not been lightened up with RADIANCE before now, we were waiting for the Delegates of The Resurrection of the Kingdom of Ethiopia.

Chapter 5

# THE BOOK'S COMPOUND LIMPED COVER

The Book's cover is Limped.
The compound impression is the Heart's
Block impression.
The name of the Book is:
Ethiopia's Bible-Text and Rule Book,
No.1. (a). Black Supremacy, by His
Majesty The King of Kings. (b).
Special Notice

I am His and Her Majesty King Alpha and
Queen Omega,    Our Work is strictly
PERFECT.

c.    We are not business with Angle-
Militant Nakedness.

d.  His and Her  Triumphant Dynasty,
   Queen Lula May Fitz Balintine
     Pettersburgh, Owner of Black
     Supremacy,
K.A.Q.O.K.O.K.A.B.C.S.J.W.

## Chapter 6

### OBEAH

A Balm yard is not a Hospital
Neither is it an Obeah Shop
Peoples that is guilty of Obeah must not
visit a Balm Yard Nor in the Assembly of
Black Supremacy.

No admittance for Obeah dogs.
No admittance for FORTUNE-TELLERS and
witch and Old Hige.

None whatever, no admittance for GHOST,
WITCH, Lizards.

No admittance for Alligators, Snakes,
PUSS, Crabs, Flies, Ants, Rats, and
Mice, and LODESTONES, and Pins and
Needles.
Jan-Crows, The Ravens, and Candles, and
Fast Cups, and Rum Bottles, and Grave
Yards are not REQUIRED.
People's Clothes, a beast HAIR, and
FOWLS and Grave Dirt not wanted.

Eleven, the Woman's Baby will strive in
HER BELLY, AND YOUR snake and Lizard
will not be able to hurt HER.
For your Ghost will come right back to
yourself.

For this is Ethiopia Balm Yard, and we
do not have no leprosy.
For Ghost only visit the Lepers Home.
This poison is for ALL Bad Spirits, it
is No. 666 it is good for the Pope of
Rome and The Monarch of Hell's Bottom.

## Chapter 7

# ETHIOPIA'S BALM YARD POISON NO.666

You will not plant your Obeah Self, with no Man or Woman, so that they cannot get RID of you until the Obeah ROTTEN.

SCIENCE, MY Dear Obeah King, your Black and white heart Obeah factory, is up-side-down.
Take, this RANKIN Dose of Fatal deadly poison and leave for God Sake; do it quickly. (Supreme Law), K.A.Q.O.K.O.K.

You will not Bline, give big foot or sore, or turn any child ACROSS the Woman's Belly, and Kill her Baby when it is born, or any time after. You will not be there to GRUDGE or OBEAH or rob the people. Nor breed up the Young girls, and treat them like dogs.
Every good looking man's Wife you see, you want to cohabit with her, you rotten GUT SNAKE.
Anywhere a man put a Business, you go there to Kill and Drive Him away, you DEAD COLD HORSE.
This pole is Black Supremacy, King Alpha and Queen Omega.

## Chapter 8

# PERFECT BAPTISM UNDER WATER

Black Supremacy, The Church Triumphant is Perfect Baptism, K.A.Q.O.
We fully appreciate the Baptism of Black Supremacy, Our Triumph over white Supremacy, Our SLAVE MASTER.
His and Her Majesty KING ALPHA and QUEEN OMEGA The King of Kings, KNEW The Perfect Value of Holy Baptism UNDER Water, and they taught us how to appreciate The Power of Holy Baptism.
Now Ethiopia and Africa and Egypt and Vast Creation of Black Supremacy will plant their seeds on the Soil of Black Supremacy.
And we have no Pardon to beg white supremacy, no favors to ask her, for she is an ACKNOWLEDGE Deceiver.
From B.C. 4004 to A.D. Second Score, she faked all Christianity.
Black Supremacy The Church Triumphant have Denounced Her openly.
Baptism is a very important Subject to Black Supremacy . Ethiopia is a Baptized Dynasty.

Every Black Man and Woman is Black Supremacy, and must Rush his and her BAPTISM. His and Her Biblical Sovereign Queen Lula May Fitz Balintine Pettersburgh, King of Kings.

## Chapter 9

# *PERFECT BAPTISM UNDER WATER*

Ethiopia is The Dynasty that we have RESURRECTED and baptized INTO Her Own Legal and Divine Body.

According to the Ancient Order, His Majesty King Milchisedec and Her Majesty Queen BEULAH *(3)* - That is to-day, Queen Lula May Fitz Balintine Pettersburgh Equinoctial Equinox. The owner of The Land of Corn and Wine. Sacred Songs and Solos, No. 277. The Monarch Songs Book of the World.

---

*(3)* 'Beulah (married) was Isiah's name for The Promised Land after the Babylonian captivity (Isa. 62:4 "thou shalt no more be termed forsaken, neither shall thy land any more be termed Desolate; but thou shalt be called Hephzibah, and thy land Beulah; for the Lord delighteth in thee, and thy land shall be married")

22

Having on the Heart, and my Egyptian
Crown and Royal Wrap SAME way A. Al.
COPYWRIGHT.
So Ethiopia must find The Virgin Mary
and Joseph and Jesus Christ and John The
Baptist, my wife and Children, of my Own
Bodily Loins.
They are all Black Peoples, I, Myself,
is His Majesty King Melchisedec, The
Said Alpha and Omega, The King of Kings.

To be baptized, in the River NILE, or MY
Powerful RIVER JORDAN.
Like as unto Lady Beulah  in the Nile,
and Lawyer Jesus in the Jordan, is King
Alpha and Queen Omega.  RIVER BAPTISM,
means the Control of The City, as a
City, must be Built on a RIVER, Like
Egypt The NILE RIVER.

## Chapter 10

# PERFECT BAPTISM UNDER WATER

Palestine My ROYAL JORDON.
Notice the Cities and Rivers of the New
World.
(To wait at, and on, "POOLS Baptism" in
CHURCH BUILDINGS. That is White People's
Leprosy.)

Angle-Militant-Adam-Abraham-Angle-Saxon
The Leper. To be Baptized into any of my
furious Oceans, ANYWHERE about the
Bar of LADY CREATION, is Black
Supremacy.

Therefore, all Adamic Abrahamic and
Anglo-Saxon "Baptist Churches, "has to
WASH Their Hands and Souls, Minds and
Hearts from Adam-Abraham-Angle-Saxon,
The LEPROUS-PREACHER.

In Countries where it is sometimes COLD,
peoples must not be foolish, Jesus
Christ WALKED over Sixty Miles to River
Jordan to
John The Baptist.

When The Ethiopian EUNOCH The BANK
MASTER, got to The River, He ASKED
"Philip" to Baptize Him. Dump up those
Hell-Holes in Churches Called Pools, and
Baptize in the River or The Ocean. The
Church Triumphant Black Supremacy.
WORLD'S CAPITAL.

## Chapter 11

# HIS AND HER MAJESTY KING ALPHA AND QUEEN OMEGA, MARRIAGE DIPLOMA

The Church Triumphant is Black Supremacy.
Affidavit, Our Live Eternal Creator, Creator and Almighty God, Crown Arch-Creator of Life.

### TERRESTRIAL AFFIDAVIT

His and Her Arch-Supremacy of Holy Time, Lover's Firmament and Penetrating, Renovator, Controller, Head and Pillow-Monarch-Groom
and Lion-Hearted Virgin Bride.
The Lion and His Lioness, The Greatest Majestic Tri-Virgin Queen Lula May Fitz Balintine Pettersburgh Equinoctial-Equinoxes.

Holy Marriage Finger, is Lady Pettersburgh's Right Monarch finger.
Head and Pillow Copyright, I can't hurt her, and she cannot hurt me, for we are The Equinoctial-Equinoxes, the Biblical Equator.
Our Professions are, We are The Owner of Communication and Money Mint, Owner of The Human Race, and Operator of Dynasties and
Bible House, and Dictionaries.
Mediator, and Crown Head of the Church Triumphant and Black Supremacy.

## Chapter 12

# THE HOLY CEREMONY OF THE MORTALS

THE HOLY CEREMONY OF THE MORTALS.

This Triumphant Ceremony, is the Perfect Copy of His and Her Arch Majesty King Alpha and Queen Omega. The Perfect Owner of Black Supremacy and Matrimony. ETHIOPIA'S PERFECT WEDLOCK. His and Her Dynasty, Queen Lula May Fitz Balintine Pettersburgh King of Kings, is the Copyright and FOUNDER of the Ethiopian Virgin Dynasty, YOUR WEDLOCK.

She cannot hurt him, and He cannot hurt her. She can have him, and He can have her on the Train of Time, for they are HEAD and
Pillow, heart and SOUL Companion for life.

The Church Triumphant, and Black Supremacy, has nothing at all to do with white supremacy, and the church militant, MARRIED IS EASED talk.

Adam, The Leper, and Abraham the Lunatic, are the Directors of the Marriage Proclamation of the Church Militant and White Supremacy. RICHER for POORER, BETTER FOR WORST, UNTIL DEATH. That is white supremacy's Marriage Solemnization. Adam The Leper, and Abraham The Indomitable.

Chapter 13

# CEREMONY OF THE MORTALS

MORTALS, you follow me, I will show you where the Marriage Office is Perfect Ceremony, is Black Supremacy.
"The Monarch Finger" on your (Right Limb is, Holy Union's finger).
Both (male and Female), will stand-facing Each other at the Matrimonial Tribunal, and The Marriage Officer will (Read) to them My (Perfect Crown Document).

And say to my Guest, According to The Perfect Copy, of His and Her Arch Majesty King Alpha.
You are now equal, HEAD and Pillow-Heart and SOUL Life-HOLD COMPANION.

She cannot hurt you, and you cannot hurt her, she cannot leave you on Earth, and you cannot get to Heaven without her.
Your ring is an emblem of Loyalty, To The Perfect Tree of Life.

Thus saith Our Creator The Living God.
By Perfect Ceremony, The Church Triumphant and Black Supremacy.
A Royal Child Christmas Gift.
(9.O.C.NIGHT) FROM THE CIRCLE THRONE THE KING OF KINGS.

## Chapter 14

## *FASTING -HOW TO FAST*

I am His Majesty King Alpha, The King of
Kings, The Copyright of Creation, The
First and The Last.
Blessed are they that SEARCHETH the DEEP
THINGS ON THE TREE OF LIFE for my Wisdom
is DEEP and is past finding Out.
Thus Saith the Living God, Owner of
Life.
To Over Come White Bondage and filth and
Black Hypocrisy, amongst your Own Black
Skin, you HAVE TO FAST HARD.
For the white man is very filthy, and
The Black man is an Hypocrite.

An Hypocrite means a crook, a filthy man
is that class of White Folks that cuts
with the Crook.
They are called black white.
Ye are the light and Salt of this and
Other Worlds. Always have a BASIN of
FINE OR COARSE SALT on your Fast TABLE
as long as God is your RULER.

When you break your fast do not THROW
the WATER over your heads, the trouble
will fall on you.

When you are all ready, with your Cup in
your hand, the ELDER WILL ASK "IS IT ALL
WELL"!
Every body shall say together, "all is
well with me". Then the Elder shall ask
again, "who will bear a true witness for
the Tree of Life"?

All shall say "by the Living God I will,
God Helping Me, for Life". And The
Leader, Shall say follow me with your
Cup of Troubles, to the BURRYING PLACE
of sin and shame.

Then Every Body walk quietly and
RESPECTFULLY throw away the Water.

Then come in and wash your hands and
face in a Basin of SALT AND WATER.
Then brake your real fast and be happy,
feeling SATISFIED and REVIVED and
Lovely.

House to House Fasting is very Powerful,
it lifts the Work and REMOVES Devils
from the Homes of those in DISTRESS.

Once Per week for the General Assembly
is alright.
A LOVE Feast (Fast) every 3 or 6 months
is NEEDED.

## Chapter 15

# *THE EGYPTIAN COPYRIGHT DEPARTMENT*

His and Her Dynasty Queen Lula May Fitz Balintine Pettersburgh, K.A.Q.O., are Egyptians, The Ethiopian Kingdom Master. And the Shepherd and Mrs. Habakkuk and Lady Indiana his Mother, are Ethiopians, the former Owner of the State of Indiana, United STATES OF AMERICA.

And His Majesty King Noah The Owner of Mt. Newark, New Jersey. And Ellen Park Johnson, the Mrs. of New Orleans. And Mt. Africa, The World's Capital, the New Bible land, The Triumphant Lot is my own lot until This Day.
Slave Traders, CALLED the WORLD'S CAPITAL, Jamaica, British West Indies.

His Majesty King Joseph is Owner of the Great Sea, and Lady Pettersburgh, The Atlantic Ocean until This Day. Canada and the furious Mississippi I have no intention to give away. Neither my PEACEFUL Pacific OCEAN PLAINS as long as God Almighty Lives.

Great ARTIC and Atlantic swellings belongs to LAWYER JESUS. KING ALPHA AND QUEEN OMEGA Copyright of Holy Time, January 8th 1926.
BLACK SUPREMACY KING OF KINGS

## Chapter 16

## *SPEAKING IN DIVERS TONGUE*

Before the Adamic DEADLY DISEASES
poisoned The Human family with FALLEN
ANGLES [ANGELS] Blue MURDER.
There has been only one PERFECT
language on the FACE of the Globe.

Therefore, the Angle-Militant fallen
Angles' [Angels] tongues, are not
appreciated by His Majesty the Monarch
of Life.
Thus saith the Living God to Creation
VAST.
For they have deceived the Race [of]
man.
And have killed the Mortal SUPREME
Monarch. Heaven is no GUESSOR, long
before this World was, Heaven has BEEN
running co-trillions of CENTURIES ago.
Ethiopia's Repository will Change and
qualify the fallen Angels Deadly
POISONOUS INDOMITABLE Lying tongues.

STUPIDITY is the most they get out of
the Various tongues spoken by the
Majority.
Ninety five out of every HUNDRED do not
know what they do or say. And Ghost can
fool them at any corner. (Ruth and
Lillian) said they knew what they are
talking about.

## Chapter 17

## *SPEAKING IN TONGUES*

Professor Rogers The House of Athlyi.
One fallen Angel, told Professor Rogers,
that his name is (Douglas). And Poor
Rogers did not know, he was "The
Principal of Hell". Judge Lucifer The
Devil is no Common Theologian.
He has got PASTOR RUSSEL and Judge
Rutherford Dead. FOOLED with His
Doctrine. Called Millions Living Now,
under Adam-Abraham-Angle-Saxon The
Leper, SHALL NEVER DIE. Note: (Millions
Living now shall Never Die).

In Nineteen Twenty-two I told Judge
Rutherford he must stop preaching Lies.
The Apostle PAUL CALLED them
Principality.
The Pilot Marcus Garvey. The fallen
Angel, whose name is Lady Astonishment.
She told Pilot Garvey, That her Big
Universal Name is The Universal Negro
Improvement Association and African
Communities League.
The Pilot Believed the Angle-Militant
Upside Down Queen.
Special Notice.
I am ready to tell you, That Lady
Creation Vast is BLACK SUPREMACY. His
and Her Majesty King Alpha and Queen
Omega, are Black Dignitary. By Lady
Pettersburgh Equinoctial-Equinox Founder
of Mortal Speech.
Speak with MORTALS, not Angels, King
Alpha and Queen Omega K.O.K.

Chapter 18

# MY RAIN BOW CIRCLE THRONE

His and Her Arch Sovereign of Holy Time
Queen Lula May Fitz Balintine
Pettersburgh. Equinoctial-Equinox, Owner
of the Rain-bow. Our UNIVERSAL THRONE
must be DECKED right to the Canopy, from
my Equator, to the CIRCLE BRIDGE.

Heaven is not guessing The Eternal
Government Business. I am Philosopher,
Copyright, Lawgiver and Clergyman.
Bible Owner, Lexicographer, Surveyor
General of Creation and Owner of Money
Mint.

The Rain-Bow will not speak in this
Port, She has Her CHAMBERLOIN
[chamberlain]. His Tri-Divinity and Her
Tri-Virginity, K.A.Q.O.

THE LAWS of PERFECT RESURRECTION
The Ethiopian Crown Mrs. at Canon Port,
is a Noble Philosophist.
A Virgin must always be look for at
every Resurrection.

Wherever a King is, there must be a
VIRGIN QUEEN. Kings are not allowed to
MARRY any one but a VIRGIN QUEEN in
Order of Perfect Dynasty, a PERFECT
STANDARD.

## Chapter 19

## *ETHIOPIA'S TRIUMPHANT PROCLAMATION*

The Bible Owner, of Holy Time, DENOUNCED
The Bible Militant.
Also The Militant Dictionary.
And take off the Black Man and his
Posterities from off The Angle-Militant
SLAVE-TRAIN at Nationality.
And Planted the Church Triumphant, The
Black Supremacy on The Triumphant Soil
of the World's Capital, The New Bible
Land, The Isles of Spring.
The same Country, That The Anarchy
called, Jamaica, British West Indies.
Black Supremacy's Greatest Men and Women
are Sub-Ways and AIR-MASTERS of every
SHADE.

They Sleep in BED and Eat WITH you, and
you do not KNOW what TRIGGER your LIFE
and destiny is ON.
The Gods of Laws are my Students.

The Air you are breathing This Minute is
Mine.

The BABWIRE Eternity is Mine.
The Brim-Stone and Fire, Vulcannon is
Mine.

Every Thunder and Lightening is Mine.

I want you to know that the (indomitable

firmament is Mine.)

When I speak to her she OBEY MY ROYAL VOICE.

His and Her Majesty King Alpha and Queen Omega and Lady Pettersburgh, King of Kings.

## Chapter 20

# *THE ROYAL SWADDLING OF JESUS AND JOHN THE BAPTIST*

John The Baptist wears The Monarch's GIRDLE about his loins.

And Jesus Christ wore the Supreme Swaddling, Both loins and head.

And we, Black Supremacy, wears them The Three ways.

First on Our heads The Royal Wrap, (12 yards) King of Kings.

The MONARCH'S GIRDLE, the first to the Skin, Through the Rectum on both legs, closely fitted and all around the waist.
Both MALE
and FEMALE for life, DAY AND NIGHT.
Ethiopia must do the Same for life, and Safe-Guard your Dynasty, and Black Supremacy, The Church Triumphant, K.A.Q.O.K.O.K.

I AND MY CREATOR ARE ONE in PURPOSE, as MY Boy Jesus said he and I are one, the True Vine, and I the Husband-MAN His Tri-Divinity and Queen Lula Pettersburgh, Her Tri-Virginity My Head and Pillow companion, K.A.Q.O.K.O.K.

This is Officially called the MONARCH CROWN WRAP. Place of Writing, from the THRONE World's Capital The Bible House in The Furnace ROOM.
January 10, 1926 A.D. 2000. (4 O.C.P.M.)

## Chapter 21

## *THE LOAD-STONE LEPOR*

The Load-Stone Lepor from Nationality,
is running towards my dynasty.
Just give him Ethiopia's Balm Yard No.
666 instantly, K.A.Q.O.
Give his business to the Monarch of
Disgrace.
A Load-Stone God, left me standing,
outside the Door, just after he draw out
the last 10 in my pocket with his Load-
Stone.
No Pardon for you Rev. Load Stone *(4)*
Jesus at the Cross. Get off this Train
and Wash your SOUL is the Vengeance of
God's Eternal Wrath.

They uses Load-Stone into The Militant
Bible House, for that is a House of
Science, The Chief Obeah Shop on
Militant Precipice.
They Called themselves Scientist to
Obeah Pinnacle. Rev. Bishop Load-Stone,
Honourable and Medical Robber, dogs can
be your WIFE
and Puss can be your Self.

---

*(4)* A possible reference to Rev.Churstone
Lord of the UNIA in Kingston...

You said you deal with puss, for puss
has nine lives, but I am the Keeper of
The Tree of Life.
And all puss gutts, belongs to me.
Lepors do not dictate to me.
His and Her Monarch King Alpha and Queen
Omega. King of Kings.

## Chapter 22

# THE LAW OF RESURRECTION

According to the RULE of Resurrections
(one Race) of people must go down to
dishonour, and The Other to Honour.
CAUTION
Make your INDIVIDUAL way Straight, when
you are at THE head of AFFAIRS with GOD
for HEAVEN DO NOT PAY, every WEEK.
But your Due-bill is SURE for every
minute of your life. I am His and Her
Majesty King Alpha and Queen Omega The
Pay Master for the Terrestrial Bar.

Black Supremacy is the Queen of
Ethiopia's Triumphant Resurrection.
Africa's DESIRE is to Rebuild Solomon's
 Temple, but Solomon, is not BIG ENOUGH,
nor his FATHER DAVID to dictate  to the
Monarch of Dread Creation.

I am  Building a World's Super Capital
for The Church Triumphant, The Black
Supremacy at the World's Dam-Head.
I am the Master Builder of  Continents,
and Countries, DYNASTIES and Kingdoms on
this Earth PLAIN.I am The Perfect Royal
Head of This World, The Root of
Creation.
King Alpha and Queen Omega, The First
and The Last.

## Chapter 23

# *ETHIOPIA'S BANQUETING CHAMBER*

Lady Black Supremacy, The Church
Triumphant INVITED me into her
Royal Banqueting Universe.
May Be, you might find a Royal Lover for
your Own Heart in This Banquet, at this
LOVE SEARCHING Battle GROUND.

If you do, let us know, when it ripe.
At the Banquet in Egypt, King Solomon,
The Black Man, made love, with King
Pharaoh The Black Man's Virgin princess.

A BANQUETING CHAMBER, HAS MANY ROYAL
SECTIONS.

You may have a Thanks-Giving Banquet for
Marriage Life.

A Memorial Banquet for a Member gone to
REST.

You will also have a Banquet of Black
Supremacy.

A Banquet for CHILD'S BIRTH.

A New Home or Business, or for Sick
Recovery.

For a Friend, or, An Assembly.

For Souls Having Peace with GOD.

For New Year, Xmas and HOLIDAYS.

For Business Properties.

For Advertising your Business.

For King Alpha and Queen Omega.

A Love Banquet to The Glory of God.

## Chapter 24

### *GOVERNMENT*

Black Supremacy has taken Charge of white supremacy, K.A.Q.O. Instead of Our Saying, Civilization, hereafter we (all) shall say Black Supremacy.
Just take this Drench of INDOMITABLE Fury and Move for the Church Triumphant right from the Bridge.
Black Supremacy is the Church Triumphant.
Black Supremacy will promote the Mortals of every SHADE according to YOUR power to go.
The Black MUSEUM will open Day and Night for Life.
Education will be free, and Compulsory, to all Mortals Being.

You may go to SCHOOL UNTIL YOU DIE, if you are not an enemy to Black Supremacy and The Church Triumphant.
Men and Women can Marry Right in School if you are of a RESPECTABLE proportion of Dignity, BLACK MUST NOT MARRY WHITE NOR WHITE BLACK, "RACE ENMITY."

Always be a RESPECTFUL DIPLOMAT.

Always give an intelligent reply to every person that Approach, or write you on any subject.

Always ask for the full value, INSIDE NATURE, of any Written Subject.
Do not put your quick judgment on any person.

Confidence is not quick to move.
Just what a people are, that is just the
State of your Government.
Do not follow Court House and Doctors,
they will fake you to Death.
Do not marry any Divorce person, it is a
curse to you.
Stick to your own Wife or Husband.

Do not WATCH and PEEP your WIFE or
HUSBAND, you are only digging a grave
for your self. Do not try to let your
Wife, or Husband, or Family feel small,
because you got more College filth in
your HEAD.
Hold Them up, they are the cause of you
being what you are.

I KNOW thousands of College hogs and
dogs and PROFESSIONAL Swines!
Also some very FINE peoples.
WHO ARE THOU? STEP ON YOUR SIDE.
His Majesty King Alpha and Queen Omega
and Lady Pettersburgh. THE GOVERNMENT.

Chapter 25

# THE OWNER OF MOST HOLY THEOCRACY, K.A.Q.O.

His and Her Arch-Sovereign of Perfect Time, King Alpha and Queen Omega. The Perfect Husband and Wife Theocracy, His and Her Biblical Equinox. Her Monarch, Queen Lula May Fitz Balintine Pettersburgh, The Crown Head of Holy Time and Pay Master of Holy Theocracy, The Owner of Money Mint, and Keeper of The perfect Tree of Life. The Right Master of Terrestrial Bequest, King Alpha and Queen Omega.

The Royal Copy Queen Lula May Fitz Balintine Pettersburgh, K.A.Q.O. K.O.K.C.L.C. Surveyor, and Patten Master of BEQUEST, Ph.D.L.L.D.A.B.C.S.J.W. Post Graduate, "The Will" MASTER of CREATION.

AND OWNER of COMMUNICATION, AND ROYAL FOUNDER. World's Capital, new Bible land, The Triumphant Lot The Isles of Spring, January 11. 7.15.A.M. 1926. A.D.2000 IN THE FURNACE ROOM.

Chapter 26

## WORLD'S BUILDING

The Root and Foundation of World's
Buildings is by Communication.
Heaven is Runned by Communication.
The Wisdom of GOD DEPENDS on
Communication.
January 10, 1926, A.D. 2000, His
Monarch, Victor, Communication is Lady
Pettersburgh's First born.
And Lady Triumph the Second.
Must not be seen before, The 12. Tri-
Virgin Equinoctial Equinox.
CELESTIAL LAW A.B.C.S.J.W.K.O.K.K.A.Q.O.
January 12 (9.O.C.A.M.). WORLD'S
CAPITAL COPYRIGHT OF HOLY TIME.

TO HIS MONARCH, VICTOR, COMMUNICATION
AND HIS SISTER LADY
TRIUMPH.
I am The Monarch of Creation, Your
Perfect Father, I am writing to you to-
day before you are being CONCEIVED in
The WORLD in your Mother's Belly.

Lady Pettersburgh the Perfect Mrs. of
BLACK SUPREMACY is my Wife,
Your Mother, is a perfect lady.
I married Her, through Communication in
the copyright Department at The World's
Capital, and could not TELL what part of
the Globe, she was at the time.
And Seal Her Married Diploma behind her
Back, because she is Queen Omega and I
am His Majesty King Alpha the King of
Kings.

Chapter 27

# WORLD'S BUILDING

And up to the Hour, January 12, your Birth Day, I have not had a line from her, for the Anarchy, The Angle-Militant Supremacy, at Nationality will not allow her to Communicate with me.
For they was ruling the Port of Communication, and they will not allow her to CROSS The Angle-Militant Gulf.

Plant that as you go, from Generation to Generation, as Long as God Lives.
And She and I, are The Keepers of The Tree of Life and Creation's Wisdom and Power House, and Money Mint is Ours, for life.
And children must INHERIT their PARENTS WEALTH.

That is why they tries to Kill you in your Mother's Belly. Have nothing to do with the Anarchy: Do not allow Black Supremacy to Marry any one from white supremacy, for there is a Rock BOTTOM OFFENCE, CALLED SLAVERY in the Heart of White Folks that will come up in one NIGHT.

He will put you and his own WIFE to sleep in his bed, and let you cohabit with her all you want just to get you in.
He will worship you, just to get on top of your Belly.

Emily MCGHIE (said), white Peoples Mind is the Snake's Mind.
Before I trust a White Person, I trust a Snake.

They take your LIFE with their PRIVATE INTO YOUR PRIVATE. (Last Warning)

An Ethiopian Patriot awaits his execution with stoic courage.

Graziani the Italian war-criminal butcher-general in one of his telegrams to the Italian Parliament wrote:-

'Not one of the Ethiopians begged for their lives and each of them shouted, prior to execution, "Long live Independent Ethiopia".

Chapter 28

# GENERAL MARCUS GARVEY AND BISHOP ROGERS

Pilot Marcus Garvey, warrants the Black Slaves at Nationality to leave for the Ethiopian's Yard Limit. Through the instrument of (Lady Astonishment). PHILOSOPHICAL COMMON SWITCH. The EUROPEAN LONG-DISTANCE ITALIAN-JEWISH-ANGLO-TORPEDO. Called the Universal Negro Improvement Association and African League.

His Holiness Pope Rodgers [Rogers], The House of Athlyi, The Athlican's Piby, a good little MESSENGER. Lady G.J. Garrison *(5)* and Professor W.D. Davis, *(6)* Met me at The World's Capital With the "Little Piby". Rev. and Mrs. Charles Goodridge *(7)* is gone with the Message. Rev. W.R. Carter *(8)* and His Sister ADDE is also on the ROUTE. Professor John Wilson Bell *(9)* Doctor of Angle-Militant-Theology, was Master of Ceremony at No. 7 Bond Street, Kingston Jamaica, A.D. (1924). I was Ordained by Him for MILITANT BATTLE-FIELD.

---

*(5)* Lady G.J. Garrison
*(6)* Professor W.D. Davis
*(7)* Charles Goodridge
*(8)* Rev. W.R. Carter
*(9)* Prof. John Wilson Bell

48

But I leaped The Militant Biblical Gulf,
K.A.Q.O.K.O.K.
I poled white supremacy, That said Year.
I promoted Doctor Bell to the Rank of
Kings for the Mistake he made.

Italians proudly show-off their
Civilization by posing for their
own cameras with the Heads of
Ethiopian Patriots that they
murdered.

Chapter 29

# THE ETERNAL LAW OFFICE

HIS AND HER MAJESTY KING ALPHA AND QUEEN
OMEGA'S WEDDING, K.A.Q.O.K.O.K.
St. Matthews 25 (ten) 10th Verse *(10)*,
left words, for Me to Lock Out Adam-
Abraham-Angle-Saxon the Lepor from my
wedding's Banquet. I do not Call
Ministers for they are not working for
me, they are following Adam-Abraham-
Angle-Saxon the Lepor.

Legislators said one Man CANNOT serve
two Masters. Adam-Abraham The lepor are
Ministers and Lawyers Boss.
For all they teach and Preach about is
Adam and Eve and Abraham The Lepor.

For they do not see not (even) one Book
in The Bible, written by Adam and Eve,
or the Book of Abraham, or Book of Isaac
According to the (CLEARNESS) of This
case, there is nobody name Adam and
Eve, and Abraham The Lepor, if you want
to get away with RED HOT MURDER.
If you ever touch the Slave papers they
catch you as sure as God Lives.
S.J.W.K.A.Q.O.K.O.K.

---

*(10)* "And while they went to buy, the
bridegroom came, and they that were ready
went in with him to the Marriage; and the
door was shut."

Chapter 30

# THE SOLDIERS AT CAMP AND POLICE DEPT.

The Officers and Soldiers at Camp that has power and influence are WELL POSTED.

Their names you will not know.
Every Police Department is out there.
K.A.Q.O.K.O.K. LEGISLATORS SAID, ONE MAN CANNOT SERVE TWO MASTERS.
Ministers says they can't work with Adam and Eve, and work for His and Her Majesty King Alpha and Queen Omega the same time.

Abraham the Historian SAID DISPISE the both of them and follow him.
Lawyers said, you have got to find a fault with them.
The Judge said, LEAVE The Alpha and Omega out because they are Black and, SKIN FOR SKIN.

## Chapter 31

# *BLACK SUPREMACY'S INFANTS DIPLOMA*

Lady Pettersburgh's infant's Triumphant Diploma.
By His and Her Majesty King Alpha and Queen Omega, for Black Supremacy.

**Name.**

**Date.**          **Month**                    **Year**

**Address.**

**Mothers.**

**Age.**

**Father.**

**Age.**

**Profession.**

**Race.**

**Continent.**

**Clergyman.**

**Name of Monarch.**

Name of the Chief Lady.

Name of Chief Physician.

Name of The Arch Bishop of Creation (Not Nation.)

Name of the Chief of Education.

Name of the Owner of Communication.

Name of the Owner of Bible House and Money Mint.

## HEAVEN'S LAW BOOK

53

Chapter 32

# HIS AND HER MONARCH THE AFRICAN POTENTATE

The Lesson learnt by Slave Traders through Black Histories is well PRESERVED.
We have given Our Blood, Souls, Bodies, and Spirits to REDEEM Adam-Abraham-Angle-Saxon the white man from his DREADFUL
downfall and Leprosy, but from 4004 B.C. to A.D. SECOND SCORE at his astonishing stop.

He is STILL INFESTED with the indomitable INCURABLE accursed Deadly Diseases.
We have given him access to the Tree of Life, we gave him the Garden of Eden, we gave him Egypt, Palestine, Africa.
We gave him The Life, Soul, and Body of Jesus Christ, at the Request of the Lepor, Ciaphas, their Chief Priest. (11)
We gave them Daniel and The Body of the Black Virgin, The Mother of Jesus, and they took Joseph also.
We gave Ourselves to be Slaves for Hundreds of Years.
WE GAVE UP KING ALPHA AND QUEEN OMEGA, THE FIRST AND THE LAST.
Now we are Perfectly DISGUSTED OF THEM.
We wash our hands of THEM, for life.
                              THE POTENTATE

_____
(11) Ciaphas, their chief priest

Chapter 33

# *ETHIOPIA'S SCHOOL, COLLEGE & UNIVERSITY*

Crown Law for Schools, Colleges, and
Universities on earth.
His and Her Creative and Majestic Arch-
Sovereigns King Alpha and Queen Omega,
Pay Master of Creation. Revelation 22.
Chap 12-13 Verses *(12)*. This Lesson, and
these Lessons, are written by my own
hand from my Circle Throne, at the
Judgment Pole, December 12th 1925
A.D.2000.

Special Explanation.    His Majesty King
Alpha   and   Queen   Omega   are   not   Our
Creator HIMSELF.
They  are  Our  Creator's  PAY  MASTER  and
BOOK-KEEPER  on  the  Train  of  Holy  Time,
and  Keeper  of  the  Most  Holy  Tree  of
Life.
Our  Live  Creator  is,  the  Creator  of
Life, and Master of all.    S.S.S.S.S.
Our  Eternal  Creator,  is  Creator  and
Owner of The Perfect Tree of Life.

---

(12) "And behold, I come quickly, and my reward
is with me, to give every man according as his
works  shall  be.  I  am  Alpha  and  Omega,  the
beginning and the end, the First and the Last".

The Tri-Divinity, and Her Tri-Virginity King Alpha and Queen Omega, are Man and Wife, (commonly) called "Alpha and Omega" we are Black Peoples.

God called the First Man Alpha, and the Second Alphabet, And told us that we are (Omega). So The Trinity was IMMEDIATELY Created.
So WE USED, The Holy ALPHABET as Our Medium of Communication, that is why we are the Owner of Education, and First and Last, Communicator. S.S.S.S.
A.B.C. -X.Y.Z
Now Our First Names Alpha, and Her Alphabet, or Alpha and Omega is (Victory).

"Our Last Names, are on Our pay-roll."
Revelation 22.C. 12-13 Verses.
His and Her Triumphant Virgin Dynasty.
Queen Lula May Fitz Balintine Pettersburgh, Owner of Money Mint and Bible House and The Human Family.

Supreme Judge of Creation, and Arch Bishop of Holy Time.
Copyright Philosopher, Clergyman, Law-Giver. S.S.S.S Form of Christian Worship.

The Black Peoples Triumphant Baptist Assembly. No.1. S.S.S.S. (Certified Married Officers).
The White Peoples Baptist Brotherhood. NO. 2. S.S.S.S.

Chapter 34

# BLACK SUPREMACY'S PATTEN OFFICER

His and Her Arch Monarch Sovereign of Holy Time, King Alpha and Queen Omega. His and Her Black Supremacy, Queen Lula May Fitz Balintine Pettersburgh, Arch Bishop and Supreme Judge (Virginity and Divinity of Holy Time'·

Owner of COMMUNICATIONS and all Creations OLD AND NEW.
CREATOR of HOLY GENEALOGY, Owner of THEOCRACY LEXICOGRAPHY AND MONEY MINT.

Creator of Furious Dynasties and Kingdoms, OPPERATORS and RUNNER.
The Crown Head of Most Holy Time and Keeper of the Tree of Life and Perfect Majestic Matrimonial Sovereignty.

Mediator of Celestial and Terrestrial PERFECT CORDIAL. REGISTRATION LAW BLACK SUPREMACY, KING ALPHA & QUEEN OMEGA.

All Governments and "PROFESSIONS" must be REGISTERED in The Royal OFFICE of Black Supremacy. Starting from the World's Capital throughout, Lady Creation. All Professionals Pattern of Pure Nature, can be moved for 21 years before a New Registration is REQUIRED. HIS AND HER MONARCH BLACK SUPREMACY, Lady Pettersburgh, K.A.Q.O.,KING OF KINGS.

Chapter 35

# EVE, THE MOTHER OF EVIL

The Adamic Tree of Knowledge and Eve the
Mother of Evil. Genesis 2nd Chapter.
The Adamic Apple Tree. My dear Lepor,
your name is Adam-Abraham-Anglo-Saxon,
Apple Tree.
That looks pretty and respectable to
your eyes. Don't it?
Why: Yes indeed - GROSS Beauty is The
QUEEN IN HELL; and the Royal Lepor.

Adam and Eve, and Abraham, Anglo-Saxon
peoples' are all white.
s.s.s.s. I am his and her Arch sovereign
of Most Holy Time, His and Her
Perfect Virginity, King Alpha and Queen
Omega, His and Her Dynasty Queen Lula
May Fitz Balintine Pettersburgh, Owner
of Creation.

We are Black Supreme Crown Head of Most
Holy Time, The Pay Master and Keeper of
The Perfect Tree of Life.

We are Creators of Creation. Dynasties
and Kingdoms, Holy Genealogy and Holy
Theocracy, and Celestial and Terrestrial
Mediator if you wish to know Our
Professions.

Chapter 36

# THE ETERNAL COME BACK

King Alpha and Queen Omega's Eternal
Come Back.
His Majesty and His Wife, Queen "Bulah"
May Fitz Balintine Pettersburgh. King of
Kings. "Egyptian Chestnut" Winner. My
Dear Creation, I am His Monarch
Sovereign, Pay Master and Owner of
this World.

Just make one Eternal come Back at my
Pay Office.
Mrs. Lula May Fitz Balintine (Bulah
Pettersburgh, K.A.Q.O.)
Please "Madam", your Vehement Venerable
Pay Mrs., "My friend Omega," of Old
Alpha the Lion of Creation.
Please hand me, the "Pay Roll" and The
Militant Balance Sheet.
And your "Majesty" will mount my
Exceeding Great Circle Throne, and throw
Old Theocracy above the wheel of Holy
Time, right into
Holy Eternity, to the Lion of Alpha and
Omega. King Affidavit "O.F." "O.F." of
Forevermore."
The Militant Pay Cheque is, King Alpha
and His Wife's Eternal come Back.
The Militant Abraham is guilty of
Eternal-Leze-Majesty, S.S.S.S., A.D.
1925.

## Chapter 37

# *NONE MATRIMONIAL PROSECUTION*

CRIME OF NONE, MATRIMONIAL LEZE MAJESTY (MATRIMONIAL PROSECUTION.) (Act.) 7377. SPANISH TOWN, English Jamaica (Record Office) Adam-Abraham-Angle-Saxon, the Indomitable Lepor and his Harlot, Eve and Sarai (13), and Keturah(14) was driven out of my (Virtuous) Dynasty by myself, since B.C.4004, for fornication and THEFT.

My SACRED Chronicle, dated B.C.4004 and my Great Chronological Fifty Horse Power-Printing Press. I am that said Man that Adam-Abraham and his boy CAIN & ABLE CUT to pieces and took My Royal Printing Fifty Horse Power Press, and pattern it and call it The Chronicle Printing Press.

His "Whoredom" is Recorded in First Chronicle, 1st Chap 32, etc (15).

---

(13) Sarai, Gen; 11; 12; 20:2 (see Abraham); her death and burial, Gen. 23 Heb. 11:11; 1 Pet 3:6)

(14) Keturah, Abraham's wife, Gen 25. her children, 1 Chr. 1:32

(15) More likely a reference to 2 Chr. rather than 1 Chr.

And more than that, Adam-**Abr**aham-Angle-Saxon, was never MARRIED,
nor any That followed that **L**epor.
For up to October 17, **1925,** I requested the General Register **Of**fice in Spanish Town, Kingston, Jamai**ca,** for Adam-Abraham-Angle-Saxon "**C**ertified Marriage Officer's Diploma" ( **This** World's Strongest Document).

Reply, October 21st, 1925 **(L**etter Number 7477). Sir you request**ed me t**o send you (Certified Marriage Off**icer'**s Diploma.)
In reply to say, Ada**m-Abr**aham-Angle-Saxon-Office does not **supply** such documents.
To The Rev. Fitz Balint**ine P**ettersburgh, Ph.D,.L.L.D., October **21, 1**925. A.D., Post Script.
The Slave Owners Chil**dren,** they has a little SLIP OF PAPER in**to the** Office of Slave City Official TR**OUSERS** Pockets in the FARMS.
That is all we think **of t**heir Official Names and Denomination**s, O.K.** Notice.
That is called Non-**Matr**imonial Leze Majesty.
Supreme Action. His a**nd Her** Triumphant Dynasty, His and He**r Mo**narch Black Supremacy, Crown **Marr**iage Dynasty, of Lady Creation, King **Alpha** and Queen Omega.

Chapter 38

# HIS AND HER MAJESTY KING MELCHISZEDEK'S AFFIDAVIT

The Egyptian Supreme Lady, Lady Bulah
(16), The Royal Chestnut Winner,
Creation's Greatest Songsters, The
Lioness of Alpha and Queen Omega, is my
Head and Pillow, Heart and Soul, Wife,
if you please.
We are Black Peoples, if you please; we
are only called the Exodus, if you
please; (The Book of Exodus) is mine, if
you PLEASE.

Notice if you see Moses and Aaron and
Abraham, gave any (Strong) report of me
in their fake Bible, if you please.
I, Personally, am His Majesty King
Alpha, the King of Kings, if you please;
the World's PAY MASTER, if you please.
I am only an Eternal Government
Employee, I got REWARD for Her Majesty
Queen Omega, Wife of His Majesty King
Alpha, the King of
Kings, for Her Tri-Virginity, Creation's
Womb-Carrier.
January 3rd (5.O.C.P.M.) His work of Six
thousand years, from B.C. 4004 to
5O.C.P.M. January 3rd 1926.
The Old Testament has no Book in
Abraham's name, not even one like
(Obadiah)(17).

---

(16) Lady Bulah
(17) Obadiah

The Man with the one (tallent). Obadiah was a SLAVE in King Ahab's House, yet he could make the efforts to write one called the Book of Obadiah.
SPECIAL NOTICE
So therefore, as far as Old Testament Books are concerned from Genesis to Malachi, are (39) Work-Men and Women.
(Ruth and Queen Estha) among the men on gospel journey.
Well SINCE a man has right to pay without Work, this world can also work with pay.

Chapter 39

## *NEW TESTAMENT PORT*

There is no Book of Isaac, nor his
Father Abraham in the New Testament.
Father, most sacred and Ever Living God,
Heaven and Earth's Creator.
And there's is no "Book" in the Bible
for the Anglo-Saxon Creation, Most
Living and Eternal and Ever Living
Sovereign, Owner of Life.
Adam-Abraham-Angle-Saxon, is not
entitled to any ETERNAL.
Revelation 22, 12-13.
I am your Eternal Pay Master on the
Train of Holy Time YOUR JOINT AIR and
Keeper of The Tree of Life, Your FRIEND.

His Majesty King Alpha and Queen Omega,
His and Her Dynasty of Melchiszedek, of
Her Monarch Queen Lula May Fitz
Balintine Pettersburgh, King of Kings.
The Book of His and Her Biblical
Sovereign Queen Lula May Fitz
Pettersburgh Pay Master of Holy Time.
His Majesty King MELCHISEDEC'S AFFIDAVIT
(*18*).

---

(*18*) Melchizedeck's Affidavit

Chapter 40

# THE ETHIOPIAN PEOPLE'S ORDINATION

My dear Ethiopia, Creation Vast, is now
Ethiopian Triumphant Dynasty.
The Ethiopian is the CROWN HEAD of this
Earth Field since Heaven and Earth has
been BUILT by the Living God.
Thank and Praise the Ever Living God, as
long as Eternal Ages Roll.
We are your Parents, His and Her
Triumphant Dynasty, King Alpha and Queen
Omega, the Keepers of The TREE OF LIFE.
We are not any family at all to Adam and
Eve and Abraham and Isaac, and the
Anglo-Saxon Slave-Owners.

For that is exactly how His Majesty King
Noah the Black Monarch was DROWN at
Antediluvia by Adam-Abraham, THE
ANARCHY.
Judge Samson lost his TRIBUNAL and his
life by marrying the Philistine white
woman. See Judges 14, 15 & 16 Chapters.

See the Philistines Judges plotting out
RIDDLES with the woman how to get him.

## Chapter 41

## *NO.1. THE BIBLE EDITOR*

HIS & HER BLESSED PSALMS OF KING ALPHA AND QUEEN OMEGA.
His & Her Holy Theocracy, His & Her Psalmist, The Head of the World.
His Tri-Divinity & Her Tri-Virginity Queen Lula May Fitz Balintine Pettersburgh of Holy Theocracy.
MY DEAR TREE OF LIFE, DEAR HEART, My True-Hearted Wife, I am just ready to put Out David the Chaff, Psalm 1st Ver. 4 *(19)*.
The Owner of the Psalms, is The Blessed Virgin Mary of Alpha and Omega and MY TWO LAWFUL BLACK BOYS MY LOVE.

JOHN THE LAWGIVER & His Brother Prince Emanuel the World's Swiftest Clergyman if you please my LOVE. PSALMS NO. 2. MY DEAR MONARCH, My Love, will you Darling, be PLEASED to have (all) My Love-Letters, Business & OTHER OFFICIAL DOCUMENTS, (Set-up) in SOLID WORK in EIGHT POINT TYPES.
AND I WILL PLACE them in my PSALMS MAKING DEPARTMENT AGAIN FOR YOU THE NEW BIBLE LAND (APRIL 27,1926) A.D.2000.

------------------------

" *(19)* The ungodly are not so, but are like the chaff which the winddriveth away"

## Chapter 42

# *THE HEAD BIBLICAL INTERPRETER, OF CREATION*

The American "Rapers" Klu-Kluk-Klan and "Mob-Lynching Policy."

The (interpretation) these unfortunate ones, are the Outcome of the "Advance-Rate" on the Anglo-Saxon Slave Train.
"The ADVANCE-RATE" means, in time of Slavery, The White Slave Masters, committed BOISTEROUS FORNICATION with THE BLACK WOMEN that were TAKEN for Slaves.

In those Days, THE BLACK MEN had no opportunity to (RATE) that is
to Lie with white women.
Therefore, while the BLACK MEN'S BLOOD was BURNING UP IN THEIR bodies for the Sexual support of their OWN WOMEN, the White Slave Masters TOOK away all the BEST BLACK WOMEN, and COMMITTED Boisterous Fornication with them.
And called it the Advance-Rate.

That is how the 3rd Class peoples come in to the human Veins.

IN THOSE DAYS this Act was called THE Advance-Rate of white supremacy.
It is the UNIVERSAL SPIRIT OF ABUSE that manifest ITSELF that the Common-Class Black MEN are NOW Raping the common-Class white women.

Both rapers, Mob-Lynchers, and Klu-Kluk-Klangs are to be SHOT down from off the Face of GOD Almighty's Beautiful Earth. His & Her Biblical Copyright, His & Her Majesty Queen Lula May Fitz Balintine Pettersburgh, Head Biblical Interpreter of Creation.

JAH RASTAFARI inspects the printing from an automatic press in England. JAH Himself says:-

"Aware of the need for the establishment of a printing press that would promote the growth of our Country's literacy and educational efforts,We establish on Maskaram 3rd, 1914 the Berhanena Selam Printing Press from Our own privy purse."

## Chapter 43

# THE MAN BEFORE ADAM WAS

I am  His Majesty King Alpha The King
of Kings, alone with my Own BONA FIDE
Lion-Hearted Wife Queen Omega, THE
BIBLICAL
SOVEREIGN OF THIS WORLD.
We are Black Peoples if you please.
The Copyright of this World if you
Please!!.
Race & Nations, Languages & Tongues &
other peoples, will come and go, from
off the FACE of this EARTH BUT His
Majesty King Alpha and His Wife Queen
Omega, We be here always if you please.

Alpha & Omega, The Black man & his wife,
was here on Earth before Adam and Eve &
ABARAHAM & Anglo-Saxon if you please.
And we, that is Our SEEDS will be here,
in gross PROSPERITY as SOON AS THE
ANGLO-SAXON PEOPLES ALL DIE OUT IF YOU
PLEASE.
We are the Type-Setters for Time and
Eternity, if you please.

Our appointment is an Eternal
Appointment if you please.
We are THE Keeper of the Tree of Life if
you please.
We are the Owner of the Zodiac if you
please.
We are The Ethiopian Kingdom Owner if
you please.

We are His & Her Register General of Black Supremacy if you please.
Adam-Abraham-Angle-Saxon The Lepor, has no PLACE in this World, if you please.
Sign The Copyright of Creation. The Monarch F.B. Pettersburgh
A.B.C., M.A.

Chapter 44

# MY ROYAL MOTHER

My Mother Mrs. Ellen (Park) Johnson of Pettersburgh, is my Virgin Mother; "this is to-day........"

She is that Royal Woman, that Landed me, The Monarch of Creation, on the SOIL of the Worlds Capital, Mt. Africa The Isles of Radiant Spring, the Triumphant Lot the New BIBLE Land.

Gross CREDIT IS DUE to the Black Peoples for such an indomitable Supreme drive. Run to the Head of the World and STOP THE GIRL that can do IT right, and drench HER from the Eternal Power-House of Human Gravity.

I GUARANTEE This WORLD, that My Wife, Lady Pettersburgh, will Land greater Men and Women than My Mother. Because she has gotten a FIERCER DRENCH and a Rapider POWER on the Wheel of Time. I have Just given my wife a FURIOUS Drench of BOISTEROUS RAGING Life: because we are the Equinoctial Equinox.

This Drench is called Genealogical Bottom. HIS & HER COPYRIGHT MOTHER-HOOD the Monarch Fitz Balintine Pettersburgh Kiⁿ j of Kings. BRIDEL YOUR CHILDREN BEFORE YOU ARE MARRIED.

## Chapter 45

# *THE FOUNDER'S SUPPORT FUNDS*

The Register General Office of
Terrestrial Bequest.
K.A.Q.O.K.O.K.A.B.C.S.J.W.
His & Her Terrestrial Bequest Queen
Lula May Fitz Balintine Pettersburgh,
Owner of the Holy Terrestrial Bar
(Wills) & all Legal Bequests.
A.B.C.K.A.D.O.K.O.K.S.G.C.,       Ph.D.,
L.L.D.,S.J.W.C.D. P.M.O.H.T. K.O.T.T.L.
Phol.C.L.C.

The Registered General Law Courts of
Black Supremacy. The Church Triumphant,
K.A.Q.O.K.O.K.A.B.C.,S.J.W.,Ph.D.,
L.L.D., S.G.C.P.G.P.-M.O.H.T. Copyright,
Lawgiver, Clergyman.
By His & Her Arch Monarch of Holy Time,
Queen Lula May Fitz Balintine
Pettersburgh Equinoctial Equinox,
S.J.W., K.A.Q.O.K.O.K.A.B.C. HEAD OF
THIS WORLD & OWNER of MONEY MINT, HOLY
THEOCRACY COMMUNICATION and DREAD
LEXIUM(LEXICON) the FIRST & THE LAST.
THE REGISTERED GENERAL DEPARTMENT OF THE
FOUNDER'S SUPPORT FUND K.O.K.
It is just, that Black Supremacy The
Church Triumphant SUPPORT. The
Foundationer from each Department,
Whenever possible, His & Her
Foundationer Queen Lula May Fitz
Balintine Pettersburgh, K.A.Q.O.

## Chapter 46

# *REGISTERED LIBRARY*

Librarian's Register General Office of Black Supremacy, A.B.C.S.J.W.
Our Creative Sovereign of Mortal Libraries of Holy Time, The Lion & His Lioness of Alpha and Omega Queen Lula May Fitz BALINTINE PETTERSBURGH OWNER OF MORTAL LIBRARIES BLACK FOLKS. The Royal Head oh the Church Triumphant, & The Eternal Angelic Hosts.

The Register General's Office of Communication by Black Supremacy the Great Triumphant Church K.A.Q.O.K.O.K.,

A.B.C.,S.J.W.,S.G.C.
P.M.O.H.T.K.O.,T.T.L.C.L.C.
The Registered Business & Authorityship, of Black Supremacy. This instrument protect the two sides of Authorityship, height and depth. The preference is always thrown over to the Church Triumphant. K.A.Q.O.S.J.W.K.O.K.

The Denouncement of the Militant Bible-Lands and Militant Dynasty. Any one found with any History, Record, or Books, or Bible from ADAM to Anglo-Saxon is guilty of Leze-Majesty, and is DEALT WITH AS SUCH. By the Dread Order of the Church Triumphant.
ETERNAL AFFIDAVIT.

The Register General Office, of The Triumphant Dynasty Great Black Supremacy.
By His & Her Copyright Queen Lula May Fitz Balintine Pettersburgh Owner of the Triumphant Dynasty & Great Black Supremacy. K.A.Q.O.K. O.K.C.L.C.

## Chapter 47

# THE AFRICAN QUESTION

The African Question is this, The Continent of Africa Proper is a National Woman.

She is that Rich National Woman that has Charmed the Men of Nations to Lie With Her.

AND AFTER A TIME WHEN THEY ALL HAVE LIVED AND COHABITED WITH HER THEY ALL BROKE HER DOWN & LEAVE HER & PERSECUTE HER.

That is just how all Nations manage to SOKE through the AFRICAN WOMANHOOD of Prosperity.

She had too much Sympathy for the perishing Nations, whose Lives are Riotously Lived until this day.

SLAVE TRADERS WENT INTO AFRICA AND DAMAGED her Seeds, beyond any EARTHLY CURE.

BECAUSE SHE HAD TOO MUCH SYMPATHY FOR WILFULL IDLERS of Various Nations. SO THEY WENT INTO HER AND ROBBED her Lands, Money, and took her seeds, to be slaves.

That to-day she and her children have no Power in Her own Land, nor ABROAD.

## AFRICAN CIVILIZATION.

All the African is to do now, Build a New.
Get out a New Dictionary & a New Bible & a New Board of Education, & a New Money Mint.

AND THE NEW OUTFIT SHALL BE CALLED BLACK SUPREMACY.
Signed by His & Her Majesty Queen Lula May Fitz Balintine Pettersburgh HEAD OF THIS WORLD.

## Chapter 47 a.

# *ATLAS SURVAYOR*

Owing to the long Delay, of my BIBLE ATLAS SURVAYOR, and other DIFFICULTIES with the Engraving Department on this side of the Globe!!!
I had to alter the ENTIRE CONSTRUCTION of the CANON.
Therefore 70, Seventy chapters are left out of this Volume.
Those you will get in One Full volume, as soon as Our Survayor & Atlas Engravers, can get through their work.

Has the Royal Honour to be, your Biblical Architect. His & Her ARCHITECT Queen Lula May Fitz Balintine Pettersburgh, A.B.C., S.J.W.K.O.K.A.Q.O. ATLAS SURVAYORS. June 1st 1926. ETHIOPIAN BIBLE PIONEER.
P.S. - The entire Bible Scroll of Black Supremacy The Church Triumphant - and all the ROYAL DOCUMENTS Along with 76 chapters of The New Canon was destroyed by a MAD BRAINED REVIVAL man CALLED ALEXANDER HABAKKUK COOMBS and his Wife.

It is impossible for such a man to ESCAPE punishment because his acts are WILFULL.
The Rev. Fitz Balintine Pettersburgh (Lawgiver) and Clergyman.

Chapter 48

# THE MAP-MAKING & BIBLE ATLAS SURVAYOR

Owing to The Militant Objections to the Rise of the Church Triumphant, We had to have DETAINED Map-Making & Atlas Work, for much important Reasons.
The ENGRAVING Department, and The Atlas & Map-Making Philosopher, had much diffuculties with the Militant Power in the New Bible Land.
I, being The Triumphant Architect of the Church Triumphant I had UNTOLD Difficulties with the GENERATION of the 20th Century.

They were all, being Stung with the Sting of Death & SHAME and were not ABLE to APPRECIATE THE POWER OF LIFE.

Several groups of Books have been destroyed by the Militant Dread-nought in Different Continents of the Globe.
A great deal of Money has been lost, by TRUSTING it into the Hands of dishonest peoples.
THIS CODE is CALLED The Register Office of Black Supremacy.
Educated Men of ALL SHADES of Learning, are WANTED with money and without money.
The same is applied to Women and Young people.

THE VEHEMENT VENERABLE
FITZ BALINTINE PETTERSBURGH
REGISTER GENERAL of BLACK SUPREMACY.
K.A.Q.O.K. O.K.S.J.W.A.B.C., L.L.D.

Chapter 48 a.

# OWNER OF THE ZODIAC

THE REGISTER GENERAL OFFICE OF ASTROLOGY, BY THE KING OF KINGS, OWNER OF THE ZODIAC.

His & Her Monarch of Renown Queen Lula May Fitz Balintine Pettersburgh King of Kings, Equinoctial Equinox, Head of This World, Owner of the Zodiac, K.A.Q.O.K.O.K.,Ph.D., L.L.D., A.B.C.3.J.W.P.M.H.T.K.O.T .T.O.L. P.C.C.L.
All Astrologers by Compulsory Must be Registered at the Register Office of Astrology, by order of the Owner of the Zodiac.
Astrologers are all guilty of the Crime of Genealogical, Sexual, Mortal Suicide. They have read the Signs of The Zodiac to suite white supremacy, the Grand Whore of this World.

They have Transfigured the Adamic - Serpent into a tip-top Astrological Master Scorpion and planted the Beast right into the ROOT of the PRIVATE OF THE ZODIAC.

We The Head of This Earth and Other Worlds, are not (responsible) for Astrological Stupidity and White Rulers ignorance.
God Almighty is INSULTED by ASTROLOGERS.
 Also all soundly thinking Human Beings on the Train of Time.

Chapter 49

# PSALM 50 BY THE MONARCH PETTERSBURGH

Psalms are the Music of the TREE of life.
THE TREE of the Zodiac was much DISHONOURED by Angle-MILITANT Astrologers.

His & Her Supreme Registered crown Manuscript of the Great Zodiac of His Majesty King Alpha and his Wife, Queen Omega, the Lion and his Lioness, Pettersburgh and His Wife Lula; Owner of the Canopy.
Their Superior Registered Manuscript of all Angle-Militant Works.
Planted a CROWNED CAPITAL of MOST HOLY CREATION, CALLED MT. AFRICA.

THE CANOPY OF THE MOST HOLY & LIVING GOD OF BOISTEROUS LOVE.
Deeper and Sounder than the Anglo-Saxon (Slave) Manuscript at the Monistry of St. Augustine at English Canterbury, since A.D.1000.

SWEET HEART, GREAT BLACK SUPREMACY YOUR TRUE LOVER TOOK DOWN The Angle-Militant Slaves, The Twentieth Century, A.D.2000.

I am the Supreme Judge of Holy Time,
Angle-Militant Crime Against the TRUE
and Most Holy Creator, is Eternal Leze
Majesty.

MY SON, THE PSALMIST DAVID ASK ME TO
CLOSE UP THE PIT FOR HIM.
I am YOUR Vehement Venerable Psalmist
and Bible Editor of the TREE of Life,
PETTERSBURGH THE MONARCH of Creation
(from the Throne) June 2, 1926.

Chapter 50

# THE THEOLOGICAL LAWGIVER OF CREATION

TO THE BAR OF MOST HOLY THEOLOGY.
MY DEAR THEOLOGY, I AM YOUR PAST
EXCEEDING DREAD CREATOR AND BIBLICAL
SOVEREIGN.

I am the Man before Adam and Eve and
Abraham the Anglo-Saxon.
I am His Arch Sovereign of Most Holy
Time, King Alpha, the King of Kings.

My wife, your Arch Sovereign Queen
Omega, Her Tri-Virginity and Myself His
Tri-Divinity, We have given Our Names
according to Bible Law.

FROM THE NEW TESTAMENT CODE, The
Revelation of John the Divine.
We came down on the Anglo-Saxon Slave
Train, in order that we could get to
have crossed the Militant Gulf at the
Gate-way of Nationality.

Now nations time is up, for National
Rulership, they must give way to the
POWER HOUSE of THE Great Black
Supremacy. The Church Triumphant.

Therefore, all Theological PLANTS, must
be RENOVATED, TO BE ABLE TO FACE THE
VULCAN of The Church Triumphant.

Theology, my love, call or WRITE to the

Registered Office of Holy Theology at
the World's Capital for your New
THEOLOGICAL Diploma.
His and Her Arch-Groom and Bride Queen
Lula May Fitz Balintine Pettersburgh:
Biblical Arch-Sovereign, Equinoctial
Equinox, Owner of the Zodiac and
communication.
Black Supremacy Perfect Parchment
Scroll, Holy Theocracy Most Dread Copy
number 5 K.A.Q.O.K.O.K.

This Powerful Canon is the Narrative of
His and Her Dynasty Queen Lula May Fitz
Balintine Pettersburgh, A,.B.C.S.J.W.
KING OF KINGS.
We are not RELATED to Militant Genesis
Pentatouch Apocrypha, Romanic or
Scientific Blue-Murder.

The Perfect Diploma. Number ONE IS OUR
LIVE LINE TWIXT TIME AND ETERNITY:
ETHIOPIAN PARCHMENT SCROLL.


1. DIPLOMA

The Bible Owner is THE Black Man.
The Bible's Supreme Name is Holy
Theocracy and Lady Diety [Deity],
Creation's SUPREMACY.

Copyright of Creation, Creator of
Dynasties and Governments, Marriage
Officer, Supreme Judge, Lawgiver, and
Paymaster of Holy Time.

Pen and Power Master and Founder of Holy

Communication and Owner of the Human Family.

The Monarch Finger on the Right Limb, is Holy Union's Perfect finger.

"My Diploma," is The Human Race, Theocracy, and Dictionary in One.

The Twelve months of the year are my (12) Degrees, "Celestial Diploma."

I am The Holy Bible's Owner, therefore, I have taken away the Adamic, imperfect (version) that is (dated) B.C.4004 and closed A.D.96.

And give to Creation, my perfect Husband and Wife's Theocracy (dated) A.D.1925 AND 26.

Clear God the Father's Perfect Reputation and The Tree of Life.

Equinoctial Equinox.

To Her Arch Majesty, the Lioness, Her Ethiopian Tri-Virginity, of Alpha and Omega Queen Lula May Fitz Balintine Pettersburgh Equinoctial Equinox, K.A.Q.O.

My Equator.

My dear Wife, I am your Husband King Alpha the Lion of Man.

December 1st 1925 A.D. I gave to His Majesty the Great Hector Joseph My chief Copyright Attorney at "The world's Capital" Our Matrimonial Affadavit, K.A.Q.O.

The Virgin, Equinoctial Equinox.

Now my Dear Honourable Virgin, Your Arch Majesty, Mrs. Lula May Fitz Balintine Pettersburgh Equinoctial Equinox.

Now Sweet Heart, my dear wonder, just take this Drench of Perfect Wonders and Live with me for Life.
We being the Keeper of the TREE OF LIFE.
The Terrestrial Guest Chamber.

Now Dear Heart, before we take charge of the Guest Chamber of Creation, we have to clear God the Father's Perfect Reputation and the Tree of Life.

We being the Keeper of the TREE of Life, we are requested to call up the Mental Power House of this world, and have THEIR BEST Physician to (Loose) YOUR Virgin matrix and give us a Crown Diploma of our Dignity.

December 27 1925 A.D. From the Judgment Throne by the King of Kings.
A.B.C.K.A.Q.O.K.O.K.C.L.C.S.J.W.Ph.D. L.L.D.,P.M.O.H.T.
The Chief Virgin of the Tree of Life, By Order of the Copyright of Creation.

To Creation Vast the Medical Board of creation.
His and Her Majesty King Alpha and Queen Omega Medical Practitioners, s.s.s.s., December 27 1925, 9 O.C. A.M. A.D. 2000. World's Capital.

Perfect law.- the Holy Physician. My Dear Perfect Physician, you are (Requested) by His and Her Ethiopian Triumphant Dynasty (To Loose) the Virgin Matri Her Tri-Virginity Her

Ethiopian Triumphant Dynasty, Queen Lula May Fitz Balintine Pettersburgh before she enter Her Husband's Guest Chamber. The Copyright Department of Holy Time and give to the Perfect Bar of Holy Theocracy this World's Medical Affidavit.

The most Holy Ground of Perfect Living Truth, also His Tri-Divinity. By His and Her Dynasty, the Tri-Monarch, Lady, Lula May Fitz Balintine Pettersburgh, copyright Philosopher, Physician, Clergyman and Lawgiver. S.S.S.S.

ETHIOPIA'S DYNASTY DIPLOMA, ORDINATION, PROCLAMATION AND ROYAL DOCUMENT.

His and Her Arch-Sovereign King Alpha and Queen Omega Supreme Crown Lawgiver. Crown DOCUMENT. The Royal name of this ETHIOPIAN DYNASTY is called "Black Supremacy"

Denouncement. The Angle Saxon Slave Dynasty is called white supremacy, Denounce him.

Official Order. By the Sacred Order of His Majesty, Our Live Creator the Living God, Heaven and Earth Superior.

Black Supremacy starts December 23, 7 O.C.P.M. A.D. 1925. We Cross white supremacy that Sacred Hour -for Eternal Life. And take off the Black man from off the

Anglo-Saxon Slave Train that Hour. Christianity and Civilisation is now Black Supremacy.

**NAME**

**CONTINENT**

**ADDRESS**

**BUSINESS**

**JAH RASTAFARI** speaking to a young
student at School in Ethiopia.

**JAH** Himself says:-

> "We have given priority to
> education over the various
> pressing National Tasks.
> That is why We personally
> held the portfolio of the
> Ministry of Education ...."

88

C O P I A

GOVERNO GENERALE DELL'A.O.I.

IL GOVERNATORE GENERALE DELL'A.O.I.

VICE RE D'ETIOPIA

Riconosciuta l'opportunità di stimolare mediante un premio la
cattura dei principali capi ancora ribelli

D E C R E T A

Per la cattura di BEINE' MERID e di GABREMARIAN vivi o morti è posta
la taglia di 5000 (cinquemila talleri ciascuno.-
Addis Abeba II febbraio 1937=XV°

IL GOVERNATORE GENERALE
VICE RE D'ETIOPIA
F/to Graziani

TRANSLATION OF ABOVE DOCUMENT

SUPREME COMMAND OF A.O.I. (ITALIAN EAST AFRICA)
THE GOVERNOR-GENERAL OF ITALIAN EAST AFRICA, VICEROY
OF ETHIOPIA, recognising the need to stimulate by a prize the capture
of the principal leaders now in rebellion DECREES for the capture of
BEINE' MERID* and of GABRE MARIAN, dead or alive, the reward of
5,000 (five thousand) dollars for each, Addis Ababa, February 11, 1937.—
XV Governor-General, Viceroy of Ethiopia
(Signed) GRAZIANI.

* A relative of the Emperor.

# Books from Miguel Lorne publishers and Frontline Books

- ❖ The Autobiography of Haile Sellassie: My Life and Ethiopia's Progress Volumes 1 and 2

- ❖ The Promised Key- Leonard Percival Howell

- ❖ The Rastaman Chant- Ras Miguel Lorne

- ❖ Stolen Legacy- George G.M. James

- ❖ The Two Zions- Edward Ullendorff

- ❖ From the Maroons to Marcus- Ras Sekou Tafari

- ❖ The Mission: The Life, Reign, and Character of Haile Sellassie I- Hans Wilhelm Lockot

- ❖ The World's 16 Crucified Saviors- Kersey Graves

- ❖ The Fetha Negast: The Law of Kings, Preface by HIM Haile Sellassie I

- ❖ The Bible of Bibles- Kersey Graves

- ❖ The Holy Piby A.K.A. The Blackman's Bible- Shepherd Robert Athly Rogers

- ❖ Babylon to Rastafari- Douglas R.A. Mack

- ❖ The Lion of Judah Hath Prevailed- Christine Sandford, intro by Ras Sekou S. Tafari

- ❖ Rastafari In Transition Vol I and II- Ikael Tafari, Ph.D

- ❖ Dread History- Professor Robert Hill

- ❖ A Rastafari view of Marcus Mosiah Garvey- I. Jabulani Tafari

- ❖ The Forgotten Books of Eden and The Lost Books of the Old Testament

- ❖ Haile Sellassie and the Opening of the Seven Seals- Kalin Ray Selassi

- ❖ The Ethiopians- Edward Ullendorff

- ❖ Emperor Haile Sellassie and the Rastafarians- Jah Ahkell

- ❖ The Rastafari Ible- Jahson Atiba

**InI works is totally livicated to the glory of Rastafari**